Table of Contents

List of Figures

List of Tables

Abstract

A safe, secure, and functional information network is vital in today's Air Force net centric environment. Information is more critical today than it has ever been. As more operational functions are placed in cyber space and greater computing power becomes available to everyone, keeping these networks safe and secure is an almost unattainable task. Network security entails Intrusion Detection Security, but another form of security or "insecurity" is quickly gaining attention. Honeypots allow the black hat community to attack and penetrate non-production systems. By monitoring and studying these attacks, network defenders can develop better Information Assurance tactics, techniques and procedures to defend their networks.

The ability to quickly analyze only those data packets predicted to be an exploit and disregard the remaining packets is crucial in today's overworked environment. Using an accredited honeypot, an Exploit Prediction System (EPS) is developed using a decision-tree matrix. The EPS provides an excellent tool in choosing only those data packets needing further analysis. The EPS uses as few criteria as possible for successful prediction. The log data from the honeypot is not filtered and all incoming log data is captured, interpreted and categorized.

EARLY WARNING AND PREDICTION OF INTERNET ATTACKS AND EXPLOITS

1. Introduction and Importance of Research Topic

A safe, secure and functional information network is vital in today's Air Force net centric environment. Information is more critical today than it has ever been. As more operational functions are placed in cyber space and greater computing power becomes available to everyone, keeping these networks safe and secure is an almost unattainable task. Network security entails Intrusion Detection security, but another form of security or "insecurity" is quickly gaining attention. The black hat or computer hacker community thrives on attacking and capturing systems for the sheer pleasure of it. Allowing these criminals to penetrate and capture a non-production system gives network administrators valuable information and insight on not only the next exploit about to attack their networks but also how the hackers penetrate and capture systems. These non-production systems are called honeypots and network administrators should seriously consider adding them to their Information Assurance (IA) arsenal.

1.1 Background

Network defense is the only career field in the Air Force that sees combat every single day [Bus05]. However, much of the information network defenders see is irrelevant or needs no further analysis. By narrowing the focus and time spent on log data, network defenders can more effectively scrutinize only those packets or bytes of information that may cause harm to their network. Oftentimes, the same person defending the network is also performing other non-IA tasks.

1.2 The Research Goals

The goal of this research is simple. Using an accredited honeypot, develop an Exploit Prediction System (EPS) that predicts when an exploit has been sent to the honeypot. The EPS uses a decision tree matrix with as few criteria as possible for successful prediction. The log data coming into the honeypot is not filtered and all data is captured, interpreted, and categorized.

1.3 Approach

Using an accredited honeypot and a training period, train the EPS decision matrix to recognize exploits launched against the honeypot. With the EPS, successfully predict exploits during the analysis and results stage of this research. After the research phase, determine if enough data has been collected and if the EPS proved successful. False negatives and false positives are also identified.

1.4 Summary

Information assurance is information operations that protect and defend information and information systems. Their availability, integrity, authentication, confidentiality and non-repudiation are ensured by preventing malicious logic or computer software code to be loaded onto the network. Studying and monitoring hackers on a non-production system provides valuable insight on how malicious logic or computer software code is loaded onto the production system. The rest of this document is organized as follows. Chapter 2 contains the literature review and provides background on honeypots and their uses. Chapter 3 describes the research methodology used to achieve the goals of this research. Chapter 4 details the experimental results and the screenshots of detected exploits. Finally, Chapter 5 describes conclusions drawn from this research and also identifies future areas of research.

2. Background and Literature Search

Honeypots are closely monitored and secured network decoys serving several purposes: they can distract adversaries from production machines on a network; they can provide early warning about new attack and exploitation trends; and they allow in-depth examination of adversaries during and after exploitation of a honeypot. In short, honeypots are a highly flexible security tool with numerous applications for security [Spi03a].

Honeypots, however, will not secure a network. Instead they are intended to facilitate prevention, detection or information gathering. Honeypots all share the same purpose; they are a security resource that has no production value. In other words, deployment of honeypots in a network should not adversely affect the performance of critical network services and applications.

System administrators typically defend their networks with reactive tools. Honeypots are a proactive tool. Using a honeypot, network administrators can detect and study harmful activities on a network and harden operational systems from similar attacks. Since honeypots only carry "honey" (what the attackers want to access) and have no real or operational data, any activity on the system is suspicious. Therefore, system logs can be analyzed for harmful activity more efficiently than logs with operational data.

Defensive tools for network administrators include software patches, boundary router protections, intrusion detections systems and internal system controls. Used together, these tools provide a sound defensive plan against potential attacks. However, as the blackhat community increases their skills, network administrators need to become

4

proactive. An example of a proactive approach is contained in "The Cuckoo's Egg" [Sto89] and "An Evening With Berferd" [Che01].

In "The Cuckoo's Egg", Cliff Stoll, an astronomer working as a systems administrator in 1989 for Berkeley Labs, noticed a 75-cent accounting error on his monthly audits. Upon further investigation and with very little help from government agencies, Stoll determined a hacker was entering his network from a communist country hunting for military documents and secrets (the "honey"). After nearly one-year of investigation and numerous nights of monitoring the hacker, Stoll was able to alert the KBG and finally convince United States government agencies that a spy ring dealing in large amounts of cash and cocaine had invaded his computer network.

"An Evening With Berferd" describes Bill Cheswick's of AT&T Laboratories adventures when a hacker entered their network via the infamous sendmail DEBUG hole in AT&T's Internet gateway machine in January 1991. Cheswick wanted the hacker to enter their system so AT&T could log his sessions and learn from his exploits. Due to close monitoring, any potential targets were warned in advance. Fake services (the "honey") were added to better entice the hacker. The paper chronicles the successes and failures of the hacker who was mostly interested in military targets and new machines. After about four months, the hacker was disconnected from the network. The greatest lesson learned in this case was if a hacker can log onto your system, they would acquire root access in a very short period.

Although the word "honeypot" was not used, these two readings capture the essence of honeypots. Any research endeavor into honeypots should begin by reading these books.

The genesis of organized honeypot research was the Honeynet Project. The Honeynet Project [Hon00a – Hon 04b] is a non-profit research organization of security professionals dedicated to information security. Their website provides an excellent e-mail list distributing their latest findings. The book, "Honeypots: Tracking Hackers" is an exhaustive survey into the world of honeypots operation and research [Spi03a].

2.1 Why Hackers Hack

A short time ago, the term hacker was a positive name bestowed upon people who could actually make computers work and produce the output desired. Today's definition is very different. A hacker (or attacker) is someone who wants control of your network. The motives of attackers can be surmised in the acronym MEECES: Money, Ego, Entertainment, Cause (basic ideology), Entrance to a social group and Status [Spi03b]. The various ways hackers attempt to compromise computer systems include:

Denial of Service (DOS): This attack floods the intended target (Website, IP address or network) with large amounts of hits or attempted accesses and effectively renders the website useless due to inability to transmit or receive data. Attackers first compromise hundreds or thousands of systems to fully engage this attack. The attacker uses these "owned" systems to deny service to their target. The DOS will render a Website useless; the same effect as if it were hacked and compromised. Often, many blackhats use DOS to take out other blackhats. Many hackers claim they make money by "packeting", slang for DOS attack.

BOTS (automated robots): BOTS act on the blackhat's behalf in a preprogrammed fashion. This allows blackhats to capture as many systems as possible

6

with much less effort. BOTS or automated tools are the greatest risk to the security community [Spi03a].

Credit Cards: Captured systems are used as currency in the blackhat community. Blackhats will trade captured systems for stolen credit card numbers [Hon00a].

Bragging rights: To elevate status among the blackhat community, hackers must prove their skills. The more sites captured, the higher status attained. Often hackers attack a website, change it and then secure that site to demonstrate their skill.

CPU Cycles: Worms will consume the CPU of affected machines. Consumed CPUs spend all processing power working for the attacker, making the machine useless for the intended user. The more CPU cycles gained, the greater the bragging rights and higher status.

Corporate Espionage: Business organizations may try to attack competitor systems to gain an edge in the business environment. These may be a simple DOS attack to deny the competitor's consumers access to the website. It may entail outright downloading of proprietary information. Usually, these are advanced blackhats as most of the systems attempting to be breached have skilled system administrators.

Political Motives: These types of attacks do occur. One occurred only one month after the 11 Sep 01 attacks on the World Trade Center and Pentagon. Hackers captured and defaced the website of the National Oceanic and Atmospheric Administration Center. The message simply stated there would be more attacks of this type [Mid01].

2.2 Honeypot Basics

A honeypot is a security resource whose value lies in being probed, attacked or compromised [ZZQ03]. If no one attacks a honeypot, then no data is captured. The basic assumption means any connection is suspicious since a honeypot holds no information of value. Some honeypot security goals are prevention, detection and reaction [Spi03a].

Traditional honeypots are production type and protect a target system from attack and as well as detect attacks. This type of honeypot alerts the system administrator who can then actively defend the network.

A research honeypot is used to learn new attack methods. Primarily established at universities, they provide more interactive opportunities for attackers. Effective data control must be exercised to prevent attacks from the research honeypot to other computer systems.

Honeynets are comprised of multiple honeypots and are mainly used for research purposes and are often standard production systems. Honeynets are more interactive than honeypots and resemble an actual network [ZZQ03].

Data control and data capture are the two basic requirements in all honeypots. The main tasks are luring attackers and capturing their data for further research. Data control is a must to avoid the attacker using the honeypot to attack other systems.

2.3 Defensive Countermeasures

Patches: Keeping the network secure with hotfixes, patches and service packs can be a full-time job for system administrators [MSK03]. This type of reactive maintenance must be accomplished diligently to maintain a given level of protection.

Procedures such as updating virus scanners, keeping patches current and disabling unnecessary services can prevent attackers from exploiting your network [Spi03a]. If a known exploit has been published, blackhats will use it quickly, often before the system administrators can install the patches. Patches are necessary, but are a reactive means of defending the network.

Boundary Protection: The primary equipment used to protect the information that crosses the network boundary is the boundary router [Tar04]. External routers and firewalls basically divide the organization's intranet from the Internet. Putting a web server on the Internet without installing a firewall in front of the web server is simply not done in today's security conscience environment [MSK03]. Firewalls can be either hardware or software or both. The location of the firewall and honeypot are very important. The hacker must be able to access and then transmit, albeit in a restricted way, from the hacked honeypot.

Intrusion Detection Systems (IDS): An IDS monitors all inbound and outbound traffic and searches for suspicious patterns that may indicate an attack. Some IDS's compare captured traffic with a large database of attack signatures. Attacks can be detected; however, the vast amount of traffic often causes system administrators to overlook the attacks. Furthermore, IDS systems often have a large number of false positive and false negative alerts [LLO03].

Internal System Controls: Many authentication tools on a network simply lock out an account after three failed attempts. To unlock the account, a user must physically present credentials to the system administrator. Passwords are encrypted when transmitted over the web and a strong password policy enforcement tool is often implemented. The weakest part of any network is a careless user who reveals their user ID and password. Accounts not used in a prescribed amount of time should be deleted. Temporary accounts should remain active for the least amount of time practicable.

Although this research doesn't discuss in detail the above-mentioned defensive techniques, they should be used in unison with honeypots for complete network security.

2.4 Offensive countermeasures

Honeypots: Honeypots are a relatively new technology whose primary purpose is to gather intelligence about an attacker [Hon02]. By doing so, organizations can potentially stop an attack or prevent a defense system failure. The very first honeypot was implemented at the Lawrence Berkley University Lab [Sto89]. The lab had several supercomputers and charged each user for use of the systems. When a 75-cent error appeared, an investigation revealed an unauthorized user entered the system from an unknown location. Even after months of investigation and systems monitoring, no government agency (Central Intelligence Agency, Federal Bureau of Investigation, National Security Administration and United States Air Force) was willing to provide any assistance. Even so, the hacker was tracked to a foreign city. Due to a non-digital telephone switch, the foreign telephone company needed the hacker to stay on-line for nearly two hours to determine who the attacker was.

Ultimately, several huge files the hacker wanted were provided so that he would be on-line long enough for the telephone technicians to perform a manual trace. The data, although not termed such at this time, was the "honey" for the hacker. Through previous observations, the hacker was known to be searching for military type data. So, several were created that appeared to be "top secret ultra-classified material". For example, Figure 1 contains a portion of one of the files read by the hacker [Sto89]:

Dear Major Rhodes,
    Thank you for your comments concerning access to SDINET. As you know, a Network User Identifier (NUI) is required for access to both the Classified and Unclassified SDINET. Although these NUI's are distributed from different locations, it is important that users who use both sections of the network retain the same NUI. For this reason, your command center should contact the network controllers directly. At our laboratory in Berkeley, we can easily modify your NUI, but we would prefer that you issue the appropriate request to the network controllers. Sincerely yours, Barbara Sherwin

Figure 1: Example of Honey in Cuckoo's Nest

With this letter and others similar to it, the hacker found several enticing data elements he could use to hack into the fictitious SDINET. This first honeypot allowed the hacker to reach outbound sites through his lab. However, a system was developed through which all of the hacker's activities were monitored. When the hacker was actually acquiring useful data, the data terminals would be manually shorted to induce noise over the data link that prevented the hacker from acquiring the data. The hacker acquired several user accounts and passwords from e-mail messages. And unfortunately, the hacker was also able to use several default passwords in routers that were not reset by system administrators.

2.5 Legal Issues

Determining whether honeypots are illegal is not a simple question. The advice of a competent lawyer is always prudent when honeypots are to be deployed. In [Spi03a], Richard Salgado, US Department of Justice, considered the following three legal issues:

1) Laws that restrict your right to monitor user activities,

2) Address the risk that attackers will misuse your system to harm others, and

3) If the honeypot will be used to catch and prosecute attackers, the possibility that the defendant will claim entrapment.

The Fourth Amendment (protection from unlawful search and seizure) to the US Constitution may also apply. This amendment, however, only applies to government agencies. A private entity can deploy a honeypot and monitor users without worrying about violating the Fourth Amendment [Spi03a].

The Wiretap Act forbids anyone from intercepting any communications, including electronic sniffing, unless one of their specific exceptions has been violated. Some of these exceptions include "provider protection" and "consent of a party". A computer network owner could use the "provider protection" as an argument to protect a service. Using the "consent of a party" exception as the basis for sniffing a network would involve the use of a warning banner. If you rely on a warning banner, take care to only sniff the bannered ports. Figure 2 is one example of a warning banner [Spi03a].

```
###############################################################
                   ! READ BEFORE CONTINUING!
         This system is for the use of authorized users only.
         By using this computer you are consenting to having
         All of your activity on this system monitored and
         Disclosed to others, including law enforcement.
###############################################################
```

Figure 2: Example of a Warning Banner

The Patriot Act exception expressly authorizes warrantless monitoring of hackers by the government in certain situations. In order to legally monitor or allow someone to act on the behalf of the government, the following must occur:

1) The network's owner has authorized the interception,

2) The person sniffing the network is engaged in a lawful investigation, and

3) That person has a reasonable basis to believe that intercepted communications will be relevant to the lawful investigation.

The honeypot should be strictly monitored to reduce the risk of it being used to harm others. An unattended honeypot will quickly become part of the problem trying to be corrected. If a honeypot does compromise a host, accepted procedure is to call a credible third party, such as the Computer Emergency Response Team (CERT), rather than contact the affected host directly [Mcc03c].

Entrapment is often an overstated risk for honeypot owners. Entrapment is a narrow defense a defendant can use to avoid conviction. However, entrapment can only apply when the government acted in a manner that actually caused the defendant to commit the crime [Spi03]. The entrapment doctrine doesn't apply to private honeypot owners.

2.6 Classifying Honeypots

Low-interaction honeypots collect a minimal amount of information, mainly IP headers involved in an attack [Spi03a], and work primarily by emulating systems and services [Hon04a]. These types of honeypots are easier to deploy and are usually installed with "point and click" type of software. Minimal risks are incurred, as the hacker is severely limited in his behavior. To ensure due diligence, use of the latest version of honeypot software and include all patches is warranted [Spi03a]. New attacks can be identified and IP addresses collected in certain cases [Bau02].

High-interaction honeypots, as their name indicates, are different from low-interaction. They provide entire operating systems and do not merely emulate a computer. High-interaction honeypots are real computers with real applications to attack. High-interaction honeypots capture the attacker's communications, such as internet relay chats or e-mails. Ensuring effective data control mechanisms are in place constitutes due diligence [Spi03a]. High-interaction honeypots have a very high level of risk as attackers have real operating systems that can be used to attack other systems. Furthermore, they are complex to install and must be built manually. Finally, more complexity is involved in establishing rules so attackers cannot use the system to attack other computers.

2.7 Overview of Six Honeypots

BackOfficer Friendly (BOF) is a simple and free low-interaction production honeypot designed to run on most Windows system. It is extremely easy to install, easy to configure and easy to maintain. The services are small though as it simply listens on ports with limited emulation capabilities. The security resource center provides a free download for personal use only [NFR05].

Specter is a low-interaction production honeypot commercially supported and sold by NetSec. Specter emulates different operating systems and vulnerabilities than can BOF, but less than the remaining four honeypots discussed below. It is easy to maintain and deploy with a low risk of damaging other non-honeypot sites [Spi03a].

HoneyD is an OpenSource low-interaction production honeypot designed for the Unix platform. Developed by Neils Provos in April 2002, it introduces some new concepts for honeypots [Spi03a]. It monitors networks of entire systems rather than one

14

IP address. When probes against unknown addresses occur, it assumes that address and then interacts with the attacker. HoneyD is a free technology and relatively easy to install via a command line interface. HoneyD.com provides a free download [Hon05].

Homemade honeypots are created by individuals and since no two are alike, they will range from low to high-interaction. They can be both production and research type.

ManTrap (renamed Decoy Server) is a commercial honeypot sold by Recourse (Symantec) and serves as a high-interaction production type resource. It doesn't emulate any services. It takes an operating system and creates up to four virtual operating systems. These virtual systems have the same functionality as standard production systems. Since it is a commercial product, ManTrap is extremely easy to install and maintain. It will not only capture scans and unauthorized connections, it will also detect unknown attacks, blackhat conversations or new vulnerabilities. Due to its operating system, this production or research honeypot can be used to attack other systems. One major constraint is that ManTrap is currently limited to the Solaris operating system [Sym05].

Honeynets are nothing more than a variety of standard systems deployed within a highly controlled network. This network captures all activity and decreases risk by containing the attacker's activity. The honeynets complexity lies in building the controlled network that both captures and controls all activities that are occurring in the honeypots. This complexity also makes it a very high risk. Therefore, there is little production value in honeynets and nearly all are research honeypots.

Honeynets are divided into two categories, Gen I and II. Factors such as resources, types of hackers and attacks and overall experience dictate which one to choose.

Gen I honeynets are the simpler technology to deploy [LCO03]. Developed in 1999, they are somewhat limited in data capture and data control ability. But, they are highly effective in detecting "bots" or beginner level attacks. The limitations in data control (no outbound traffic) make it fairly simple for a hacker to fingerprint or identify them as a honeynet. Since the machines are normally default installations of various operating systems, hackers do not see any "honey" to attract them.

Gen II honeynets were developed in 2002 [LCO03]. The main focus of improvement was data control. Gen I honeynets used a firewall to limit or totally block outbound connections. This is effective data control but will not attract skilled blackhats. Gen II honeynets provide data control by examining outbound traffic and determining whether to pass, block or even modify the packets to make them benign. As expected, Gen II honeynets are more complex than Gen I honeynets. Gen II honeynets can be defined as Gen I Honeynets with layer 2 devices or applications for the purpose of traffic manipulation [Tor02].

2.8 Blackhat Trends

The Honeynet Project has noticed four trends in the blackhat's tools and tactics [Hon02]. Scanning tactics are becoming increasingly aggressive. In the past, blackhats would try to identify vulnerable systems. Now the trend is to just identify a service and try to exploit it over almost any system. This thwarts the common technique of "security through obscurity".

Encryption techniques make tracking hackers much more difficult. Once a system is compromised, blackhats will use secure shell (SSH) instead of *telnet* to control the exploited system.

Rootkits essentially automate the entire process of taking control of a system. More advanced rootkits such as *Adore* modify the kernel of the operating system. The binaries of the system are not modified so programs like *Tripwire* (monitoring tool) can no longer detect when a rootkit has been installed.

The last trend is worms that not only automate the probing and attacking of systems but also are self-replicating. Traditionally, worms were limited to Windows-based systems. However, beginning in early 2001, worms such as *Ramen*, *Lion* and *Sadmind/IIS* were created to attack UNIX-based systems. The severity of worms has rapidly grown with the increasing reliance on the Internet for critical infrastructure [PSW02].

2.9 Current Research (other than the Honeynet Project)

Georgia Tech University Honeynet to Detect Exploited Systems [LLO03]

Georgia Tech University has over 20,000 students and faculty in 69 separate departments with nearly 35,000-networked computers. The average Internet throughput is 600Mbps and the network processes nearly four terabytes of data daily. The Information Security Directorate (ISD), one of seven directorates operating under the Office of Information Technology (OIT), is responsible for education on security issues,

17

assessing current policies, assisting in strengthening technical resources and developing strategies to react to incidents that affect the network.

The ISD does not run a firewall at the Internet connection to the campus. Individual departments do run firewalls tailored to their respective security requirements. The ISD does operate an IDS at the gateway to monitor known exploits. Suspicious traffic is not curtailed, but undergoes a follow-on investigation.

The Georgia Tech Gen I Honeynet was established in the summer of 2002 with open source software and equipment no longer used for production value. Initially established on one computer, it now consists of three different machines running various operating systems. OIT provided the IP address range and Georgia Tech owns it.

The *rc.firewall* script from The Honeynet Alliance established the firewall with Data Control for the honeynet. This script provides Network Address Translation (NAT) for the target machines.

SNORT is open source software that monitors the network. It is primarily signature-based with anomaly plug-ins available. The system monitors the honeynet using a Network Interface Card (NIC) set to promiscuous mode. The NIC card does not have an assigned IP address and thus the network monitoring system is invisible to the hacker. Two sessions of *SNORT* run simultaneously. One matches signatures of potential hostile activities against Honeynet bound traffic. Georgia Tech uses the Analysis Console for Intrusion Detection (ACID) developed by the CERT, which aids analysis of alerts generated by *SNORT*. The other *SNORT* session runs in packet capture mode, capturing all traffic to and from the Honeynet. The monitoring console is isolated from the honeynet network and provides data capture.

The data collected is stored in two separate locations for security. Alerts triggered by *SNORT* are stored in a SQL database and analyzed on a daily basis. The three-computer network honeynet review took at least one hour per day. *Ethereal* analyzed the data and displays the source and destination addresses, protocol used, source and destination ports and packet contents.

During the six-month experiment, this honeynet detected 16 compromised systems on the network. These included both worms, exploits and individual systems targeted and compromised by hackers. The OIT was alerted each time a compromised occurred. Sometimes the compromise was already known and other times it was unknown. This demonstrated the benefit of the honeynet.

One system's password was compromised by a hacker and then used to connect to another system. The hacker also established a backdoor to connect later. The honeynet team knew of the backdoor and diligently monitored it to observe the hacker's actions. Several days after compromising this system, the hacker returned through the backdoor to connect to another system. Without the Honeynet team, the OIT team could not have discovered the malicious user.

The lessons learned by the Georgia Tech team were [LLO03]:

1) Start small. Begin initially with a single machine.

2) Maintain good relations with your enterprise administrators. These are the people that will benefit the most from your research.

3) Focus on attacks and exploits originating from within your enterprise network. These will cause the most severe damage as they have already been compromised.

4) Don't publish the IP address range of the Honeynet.

5) Don't underestimate the amount of time required to analyze the data collected from the Honeynet. It must be examined daily and can take weeks to fully document an attack.

6) Powerful machines are not necessary to establish the Honeynet.

Connection Redirection Applied to Production Honeypots

Honeypots can be built from virtual machines. Using these virtual machines, attacks to a legitimate system are redirected to the honeypot posing as the original destination without the attacker's knowledge. Therefore,

1) Attacks against the legitimate server are neutralized,

2) The attacker is less apt to fingerprint the honeypot, and

3) Successful attacks can be studied and used to protect the legitimate server against further attacks.

The key to attack redirection is packet filtering. Packet filtering occurs numerous times as packets travel the Internet. Which criteria to filter on is the key question. For example, a key port to attack is port 80 (HTTP). If an attacker attempts the latest IIS exploit on a web server with port 80 active, the packet payload is a clear indication that this may be a malicious activity. A routing device could route this packet to the honeypot versus the production system. *SNORT* uses signature files that match characteristics of certain communications, so it is less likely the honeypot will be fingerprinted.

Once a signature is matched, the traffic is redirected from the production system to the honeynet system. *SNORT* and other IDS's are passive monitors that do not redirect traffic. *IPtables* is a robust and stateful firewall that uses *string matching* for redirection.

Consider an example of this using the file *robots.txt*. All requests for this file will be logged and an alert will be generated via rules established in the *IPTables* command. *IPTables* commands are entered via the command line.

A *SNORT Signature Rule* is then used to discover an exploit using a buffer overflow in the WebDAV component of Microsoft's IIS Web Server. Using this modified rule, the traffic will now be redirected to honeypot's IP address.

To use this redirection method, four criteria must be met [LLO03].

1) An attacker must not be aware of the routing device between him and the web server.

2) A legitimate user must not be affected at anytime. Non-malicious traffic should not be redirected.

3) A routing device must not affect the Web server and normal request must still reach the server.

4) Honeypots must be able to collect information on the attack and an attacker must not launch attacks against other systems.

Pelletier [Pel04] began tests by sending legitimate requests that reached the server with no redirection. A port scan (using *Nmap*) then tested the redirection rules. *Tcpdump* proved that the "attack" was redirected to the honeypot. The *Nmap* outputs on the attacking machine provided no indication the scan was redirected.

Basic port redirection is possible; however, there are still questions to be answered. First, TCP, unlike UDP, requires a three-way handshake. When using string matching to redirect packets, the honeypot was receiving packets that ultimately were dropped since no session was established between the sender/attacker and the honeypot.

All UDP traffic was redirected without incidence. However, only the TCP initial traffic was captured causing a non-robust solution. Attackers can quickly fingerprint this type of honeypot until more research has remedied the problem.

2.10 Summary

Honeypot's only value lies in being probed, attacked or compromised. They should not have any production value. Hackers are becoming more creative in ways to exploit computer networks and system administrators must respond. In addition to established defensive countermeasures, the honeypot provides a proactive approach to defending networks. Legal issues must be addressed in accordance with established law. In order to attract the more skillful blackhats, honeypots have moved to their second generation. These types of honeypots are more disguised and less apt to be discovered or fingerprinted. Although a new technology, current research has proven honeypots to be a viable resource for network protection.

3. *Methodology*

3.1 Problem Definition

Computer exploits and attacks have become commonplace in today's computer-dependant society. Simply connecting to the Internet exposes computer systems to attacks by hackers. Once the hacker compromises a system, it can also be used to attack other systems. Often the blackhat community is ahead of the government agencies tasked with detecting and preventing the attacks.

A computer exploit is software that takes advantage of vulnerability, leading to privilege escalation or denial of service on a computer system. A non-intrusive scan that includes a simple scan of the target system's attributes (e.g., inspecting the file system for specific files or file versions, checking the registry for specific values, scanning for missing security updates, port scanning to discover which services are listening) is not considered an exploit. Intrusive scanning actually tries to exploit the vulnerabilities the scanner is looking for.

Goals: The goal of this research is to identify exploits in incoming network traffic.

Hypothesis: Using system log data normally collected by operating systems, exploits can be recognized.

Approach: Using an accredited honeypot, system activity is collected and compared to characteristics of known exploits. A decision tree is used to recognize known exploits and identify previously unknown exploits as well.

3.2 System Boundaries

The system under test (SUT) is the Exploit Prediction System (EPS). The component under test (CUT) is the decision tree matrix. Log data, which constitute the workload to the system, arrive via the honeypot to the EPS.

The honeypot for this research is owned by the Air Force Information Warfare Center (AFIWC) and physically located in the AFIT computer laboratory. The Computer Network Defense and Response System (CNDRS) is shown in Figure 3 and serves the following Information Operations roles: intrusion profiling, computer network defense, threat response, and data forensic collection.

Figure 3: CNDRS Suite Used For Research

The CNDRS is used for computer network defense, intelligence gathering and law enforcement. This research uses the intelligence-gathering portion of the CNDRS. [AFI04a] and [AFI04b] provide much more in-depth information about the CNDRS.

The CNDRS specific components are [LM04]:

24

- Automated Security Incident Measurement (ASIM) system

  - Intrusion detection tool for monitoring Air Force networks

- CNDRS ASIM Gateway Environment (CAGE)

  - Containment and honeypot risk reduction tool

- Common Intrusion Detection Director System (CIDDS)

  - Sorts, filters and analyzes received information in real time

  - Ethereal 0.10.5 is installed on this system. Ethereal is a network traffic sniffer or a protocol analyzer. Ethereal is freely available for UNIX/Linux and Microsoft Windows from the Ethereal web site: http://www.ethereal.com

  - Ethereal is used to analyze and definitively prove exploits.

- Log Host

  - Centralized location for forensic honeypot data collection

- File Transfer Protocol (FTP) version wu-2.6.1-18 honeypot

  - Allows anonymous read only access and entices hostile intruders

  - Highest incoming log data of the AFIT CNDRS

  - The following patches are installed:

    - Openssl-0.9.6b-32.7.i686.rpm

    - Openssl095a-0.9.5a-20.7.i386.rpm

    - Openssl-perl-0.9.6b-32.7.i386 rpm

    - Openssl-devel-0.9.6b-32.7.i386 rpm

    - Openssl-0.9.6b-32.7.i386 rpm

    - Kernel-2.4.18-27.7.x.i686.rpm

- Windows 20000 Internet Information Services (IIS) version 5.0 v1.0 honeypot
  - Read only access with upload and download denial
  - 2nd highest incoming log data of the AFIT CNDRS
  - The following Microsoft patches are installed:
    - KB329115 that corrects the certificate validation flaw that could enable identity spoofing vulnerability.
    - KB823182 that corrects vulnerability in Authenticode verification.
    - KB823559 that corrects a buffer overrun in the HTML converter.
    - KB824105 that corrects a flaw in NETBIOS.
    - KB825119 that corrects a buffer overrun in Windows Help and Support Center.
    - KB826232 that corrects a buffer overrun in Windows Troubleshooter ActiveX Control.
    - KB828035 that corrects a buffer overrun in Messenger Service.
    - KB828741 that corrects the Microsoft RPC/DCOM remote shell vulnerability.
    - KB828749 that corrects a buffer overrun in the Workstation Service.

- KB837001 that corrects Microsoft Jet Database Engine vulnerability.

- Computer Hackers Area of Forensic Facades (CHAFF)

  o Virtual honeypot tool

  o 3rd highest incoming log data of the AFIT CNDRS

- False Logon w/Automated Redirection for Examination (FLARE)

  o Allows remote redirection of activity

CNDRS honeypot components are used to attract intruders. Since there is no production data on the network, there is no need to redirect the attacker(s). All attacks are directed to the honeypots. The honeypot keeps the intruders occupied while providing and collecting forensic evidence.

3.3 System Services

The EPS provides two services. First, log data is captured and analyzed. Second, a prediction of future exploits is calculated. Service outcomes are log data of exploits or merely port scans of the destination port.

3.4 Workload

The workload for the system is log data provided by the unknown black hat community. The workload characteristics include:

- Attack duration measured in seconds

- Source IP

- Destination IP

  o FTP or IIS

- Source port

- Destination port

- Bytes sent

- Bytes received

- Packets sent

- Packets received

3.5 Performance metrics of the EPS

The metrics used to measure the performance of the system include:

Success: Correctly identifying exploits.

Failure: Inability to identify possible exploits.

False negatives may occur with low and slow attacks from sophisticated hackers who penetrate the honeypot. Low and slow attacks are when a very patient attacker executes a few probes at a time over the course of days or weeks, to avoid detection. These attacks are outside the scope of this research due to time contraints.

False positives occur when AFWIC initiates a communication session to upgrade system data, to install new software or simply to monitor their system. The source IP identifies these false positives and prevents them from being identified as an exploit.

3.6 Parameters

A parameter is a characteristic of the system or workload that affects performance. The EPS parameters are:

- Source IP

- Destination IP

28

- Source port

- Destination port

- Bytes sent

- Bytes received

- Packets sent

- Packets received

- Attack duration measured in seconds

- Network Protocol

- The decision tree parameters are:

- Bytes received by the Honeypot

- Bytes sent from the Honeypot

3.7 Factors

Factors varied in this experiment are the bytes received by the honeypot and the
bytes transmitted by the honeypot. During the four-week EPS training period, these two
factors provided the best snapshot of an exploit. As this research attempts to quickly
predict an exploit, finding the least amount of factors possible weighed heavily in
designing the matrix.

3.8 Evaluation Technique

The direct measurement of a real system is used for this experiment. The AFIT
honeypot is an accredited honeypot in use for research purposes only and provides the
best means to reach the research goal.

The network topology is shown in Figure 4. The honeypots are located behind the AFIT boundary router and also have the protection of a firewall. There is no AFIT internal access to the honeypots. The only access is from outside the AFIT campus. The number of virtual honeypots is not limited by hardware availability. The VLANs connectivity allows monitoring by outside agencies and also redirection of the virtual honeypots if required. The two physical honeypots, FTP Server and IIS Web Server, do not have the guest account login feature locked out and will allow anonymous log-in.

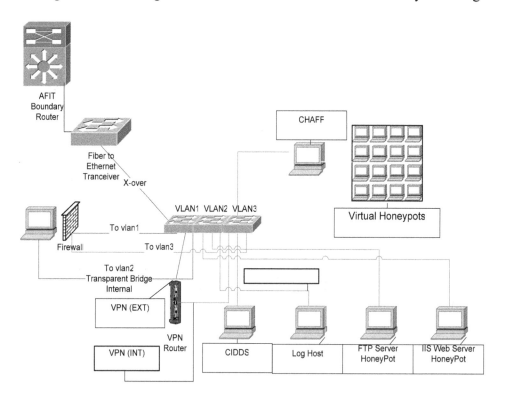

Figure 4: AFIT Honeypot Network Topology

3.9 Experimental Design

The experimental design is a full factorial design with replications. The direct measurement experiment has an unknown number of total possible captured exploits.

30

The total number of weekly possible exploits is anticipated to be over 100 [LM04]. To ensure a high number of exploits, known exploits are directed to the honeypots using a known exploit generator [Moo04].

Decision theory dictates the decision process must be trained before implementation. Metasploit [Moo04] provides known exploits to the decision tree matrix. Metasploit version 2.4 has seven different exploits against IIS systems. Of these seven, five are for services on the honeypot IIS. According to Dr. Gilbert Peterson, Assistant Professor of Engineering and Management at AFIT who specializes in decision theoretic planning, the normal percentage of events used to train a decision process is 60 – 80 percent [Pet05]. For this experiment, four of the five exploits were chosen to train the system on predicting IIS exploits.

For the FTP server, the FTPD Glob vulnerability was chosen to train the system. The problem is not a typical buffer overflow or format string vulnerability, but a combination of two bugs: an implementation of the glob command that does not properly return an error condition when interpreting the string ~ {, and then frees memory which may contain user supplied data [Sec01]. This is a well known exploit and thus selected as a training tool. Finding FTP exploits proved much more difficult to find and launch than finding IIS exploits. This training period lasted from 17 April to 14 May 2005 (four weeks). The period ended only when the EPS had been successfully trained.

The EPS Decision Tree Matrix, derived from the EPS training period, is shown in Figure 5. The decision tree has two factors. Pilot studies indicated these are good indicators of an actual exploit. By sending known exploits to the EPS and analyzing the results, the decision tree matrix was then finalized. Several possible indicators were

31

analyzed during this initial research phase. The next phase, analysis and results, should

demonstrate whether these are good indicators.

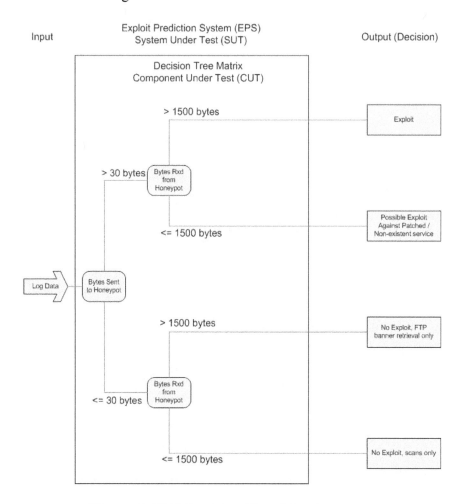

Figure 5: EPS Decision Tree Matrix

The decision tree has four different criteria to consider. The first decision is from

the "Bytes Sent to the Honeypot". From the EPS training period, the criteria of greater

than 30 bytes or less than or equal to 30 bytes was chosen. Above 30 bytes indicates an

exploit as proved during the training period. Equal to or below 30 bytes indicates there is

no exploit.

The next decision is the "Bytes Received from the Honeypot". From the EPS

training period, the criteria of above or below 1,500 bytes were chosen. Above 1,500 bytes indicates an exploit as proved during the EPS training period. Below 1,500 bytes may indicate an exploit against a patched service or non-offered service or may indicate an FTP Banner Retrieval.

The EPS training period data resulted in the decision tree matrix having one of four decisions or outputs. They are:

- Bytes Sent > 30 bytes and Bytes Rxd > 1,500 bytes indicates an exploit

- Bytes Sent > 30 bytes and Bytes Rxd ≤ 1,500 bytes indicates a possible exploit against a patched / non-resident service

- Bytes Sent ≤ 30 bytes and Bytes Rxd > 1,500 bytes indicates no exploit, but an FTP banner retrieval

- Bytes Sent ≤ 30 bytes and Bytes Rxd ≤ 1,500 bytes indicates no exploit, but a port scan.

3.10 Summary

The ability to collect and analyze detected exploits is vital for this experiment. This chapter described the goals, hypothesis and approach for the research. System boundaries, including the SUT and CUT, were discussed. The workload, performance metrics and parameters were identified. The decision tree matrix was introduced and discussed. Additionally, the analysis design and evaluation technique were discussed.

4. Analysis and Results

4.1 Introduction

The honeypot log data for this Chapter was captured from 15 May 2005 to 16 July 2005 (nine weeks). The CIDDS 3.1 navigator software provides the querying tool for this experiment. All log data coming into the IIS server and FTP server are captured by the CIDDS software. No data is filtered.

4.2 Querying the System

At the initial login screen, the "query" and "advance query" options are chosen. The advanced query page is now active as shown in Figure 6 on the following page. Options chosen for the advance query are:

- o Start Day (2005-06-26, for this particular query)

- o End Day (2005-06-29, for this particular query)

- o Source IP

- o Destination IP (either 129.28.248.27 or 129.28.248.26)

- o Source Port

- o Destination Port

- o Bytes Sent

- o Bytes Received

- o Packets Sent

- o Packets Received

- o Duration in seconds (data is ordered descending by duration)

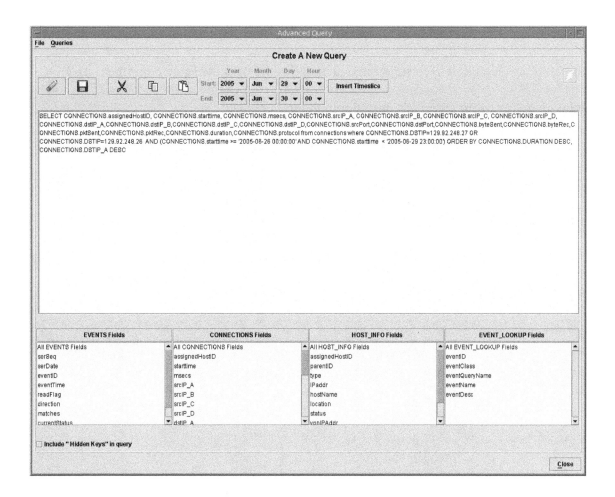

Figure 6: Advance Query

4.3 Query Results

The query results are shown in Figure 7 on the following page. Other fields in the

query results are the assigned designator – a nomenclature to identify which AFIWC

honeypot is being queried. Also, the number 6 protocol (designated by AFIWC) is

Transmission Control Protocol (TCP), which comprised nearly all of the log data. TCP is

one of the core protocols of the Internet protocol suite. Using TCP, programs on

networked computers can create connections to one another, over which they can send

data. The protocol guarantees that data sent by one endpoint will be received in the same order by the other, and without any pieces missing. It also distinguishes data for different

applications (such as a Web server and an email server) on the same computer. TCP

supports many of the Internet's most popular applications.

A small amount (4 of 8,444) of log data was number 17 (designated by AFIWC),

the Internet Security Association and Key Management Protocol (ISAKMP). ISAKMP is

a cryptographic protocol which forms the basis of the Internet Key Exchange (IKE)

protocol. IKE forms the basis for IP security (IPSEC). All captures were from within the

AFIWC network.

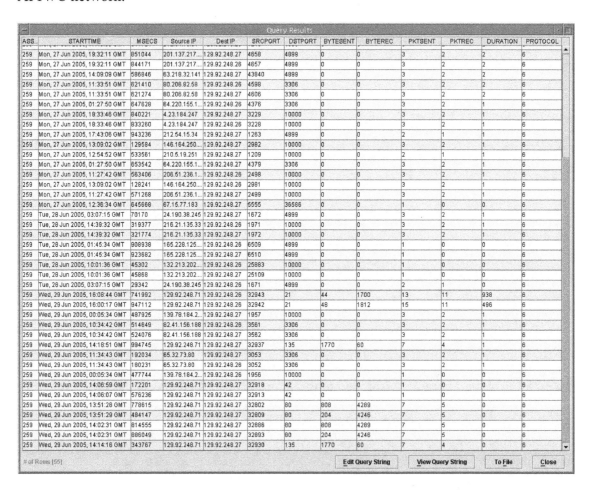

Figure 7: Query Results

Total log data captured for the nine-week period were 8,444 entries. The subset of exploits, exploits against patched / non-offered services, and FTP banner retrievals are contained in Appendix A.

The query in Figure 7 is typical of the captured log data. For this particular three-day period, there were 55 rows of captured log data. This screen shot displays 40 of these rows. An initial view of the 40 rows displayed shows 32 of the rows have "0" bytes received and "0" bytes sent. These are simple port scans to detect open ports. Six exploits meet the EPS decision tree matrix criteria for an exploit. To further investigate, the user must click on the STARTTIME for the particular log data row. Another screen is displayed, showing the transcript for the chosen log data. This transcript is an Ethereal product and is explained on the following pages.

4.4 Exploits Recognized by the EPS

The following are some exploits that were recognized by the EPS. For example, log data from 29 Jun 2005, 16:08:44 GMT is shown in Figure 8 on the following page. The left side of the transcript is the activity of the source IP or the computer attempting connection to the honeypot. The right side of the transcript is the activity from the destination IP or the honeypot computer. Data from the initiator host (bytes sent in the EPS) and data from the receiver host (bytes received in the EPS) are the truth data needed to determine if the log is an exploit. The Open Source Vulnerability Database [OSV05] and Secunia Stay Secure [Sec05] are excellent sources to verify vulnerabilities. In this example, the initiator host command "PASV" is an exploit that attempts to consume all available ports on the system by issuing multiple PASV commands. All exploits captured during this research are detailed in Appendix B. This particular exploit, PASV, was captured four times.

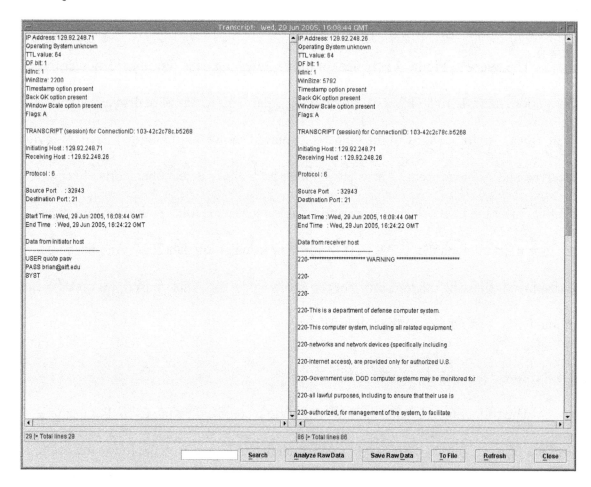

Figure 8: Captured Exploit 29 Jun 2005, 16:08:44GMT

The user can further investigate the data by clicking "Analyze Raw Data". This screen will analyze down to the packet level. Figure 9 is the raw data for this exploit. With the EPS, only those predicted exploits should be analyzed at this level.

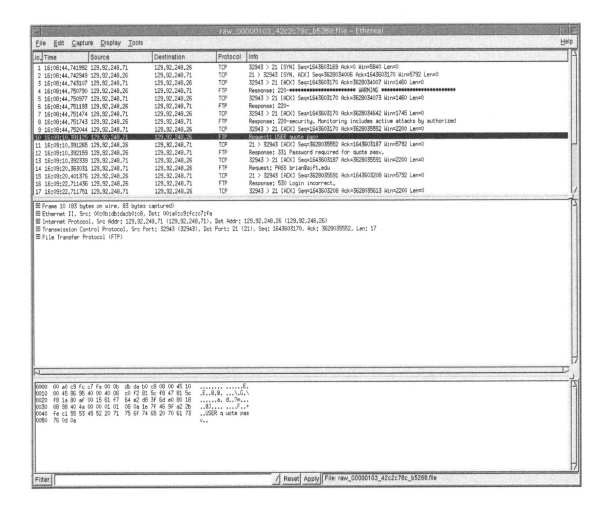

Figure 9: Packet Level Analysis

Another one of the six log data identified as exploits by the EPS in Figure 7 is the

29 Jun 2005, 13:51:28 GMT line of data. This transcript is shown in Figure 10 above and

is identical to log data 29 Jun 2005, 14:02:31GMT. This exploit is the IIS Web

Application Source Code Disclosure that attempts to dump the source code of a remote

web application using a variety of techniques. Log data line 29 Jun 2005, 13:52:28GMT

worked in unison with log data line 29 Jun 2005, 13:52:29GMT (pictured in Figure 11

below). Log data line 29 Jun 2005, 14:02:31 worked in unison also with log data line 29

Jun 2005, 14:02:31 (2). This last log data line is identical to Figure 11 and this exploit was captured six times.

4.4.1 IIS Web Application Source Code Disclosure

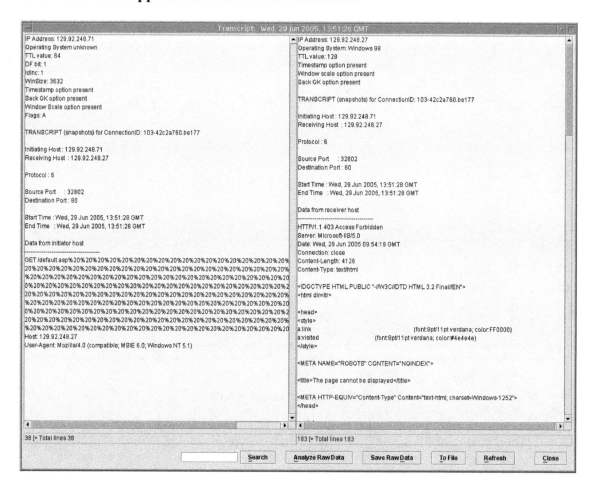

Figure 10: Captured Exploit 29 Jun 2005, 13:51:28GMT

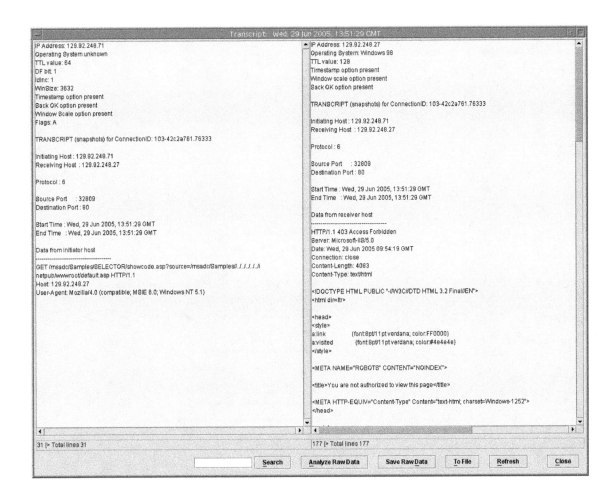

Figure 11: Captured Exploit 29 Jun 2005, 13:51:29

4.4.2   Grim's Ping

The Grim's Ping is an automatic exploit that attempts to develop tools and information for a further and more harmful attack. The exploit will attempt to log into multiple directories and perform a thorough scan of the FTP server to allow information needed for the black hat to plan future attacks. It will attempt to upload the file "space.asp", an Active Server Page that displays even more information about the host. Test files are loaded to verify the FTP server is capable of hosting an unknown site. The exploit is pictured below in Figure 12 below and was captured three times.

41

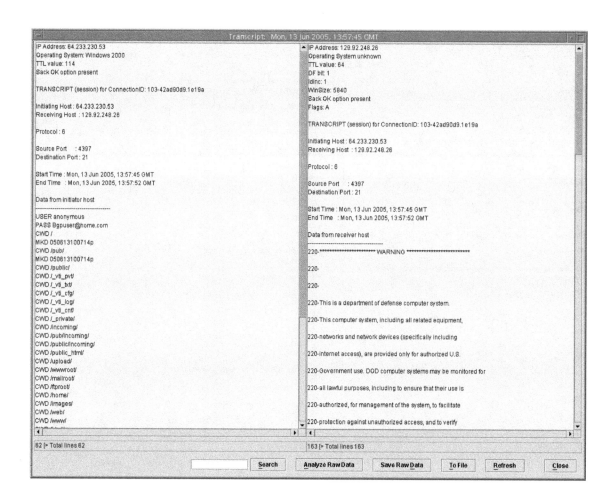

Figure 12: Captured Exploit 9 Jun 2005, 13:57:45GMT

4.4.3   IIS 4.0/5.0 .HTR Buffer Overflow

This exploit attempts a buffer overflow attack against Windows 2000 IIS 5.0 systems. This may lead to denial-of-service conditions, but will not provide an attacker with interactive access to the host system. This exploit is pictured in Figure 13 on the following page and was captured four times.

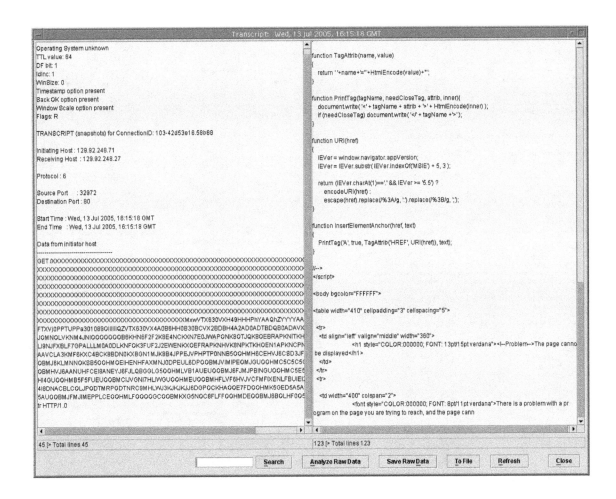

Figure 13: Captured Exploit 13 Jul 2005, 16:15:18GMT

4.4.4 IIS 5.0 Printer Buffer Overflow

This vulnerability arises when a buffer of approximately 420 bytes is sent within

the HTTP Host header for a ".printer ISAPI" request. Upon execution, a buffer overflow

occurs within IIS and the x486 instruction pointer is overwritten. Windows 2000 will

restart the web server if it has crashed. This automatic restart feature makes it easier for

remote attacks to execute code against Windows IIS 5.0 web servers. The attacker can

have the EIP jump to the exploit code and then the attacker has system level access. The

exploit is pictured in Figure 14 and was captured three times.

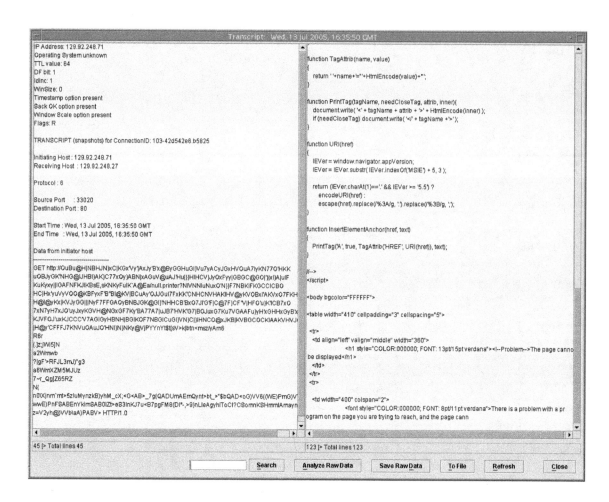

Figure 14: Captured Exploit 13 Jul 2005, 16:35:50GMT

4.4.5 OPTS "UTF8 On" Command

The "OPTS" (options) command provides ability to set options on the server. The "UTF8 On" flag sets the encoding to Uniform Transformation Format of 8 bits. UTF-8 is especially useful for transmission over 8-bit Electronic Mail systems. Although not a recognized exploit, someone attempting to change the options on the server should cause concern. This exploit is picture in Figure 15 and was captured twice.

44

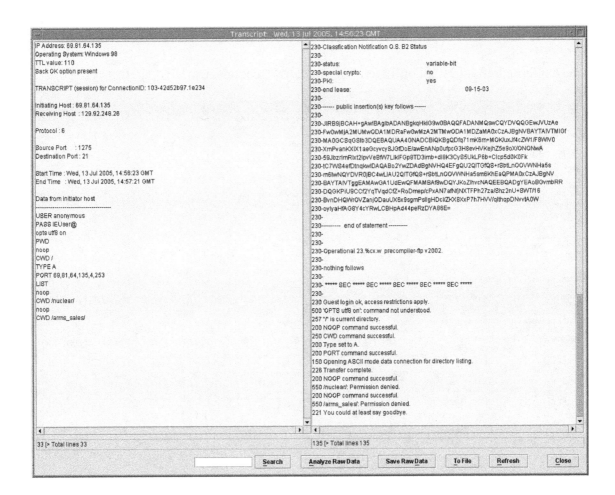

Figure 15: Captured Exploit 13 Jul 2005, 14:56:23GMT

4.5 Exploits Against Patched or Non-Offered Services

The following exploits against patched or non-offered services were captured by EPS.

4.5.1 FrontPage Exploit

A remote overflow exists in Microsoft FrontPage. The fp30reg.dll fails when handling chunked encoded data resulting in a boundary overflow and an attacker can allow execution of arbitrary code granting system level privileges. The FrontPage service is not offered on the honeypot. The exploit is pictured in Figure 16 below and was attempted 43 times, all on 13 Jul 05, spaced 58 seconds apart and against port 80.

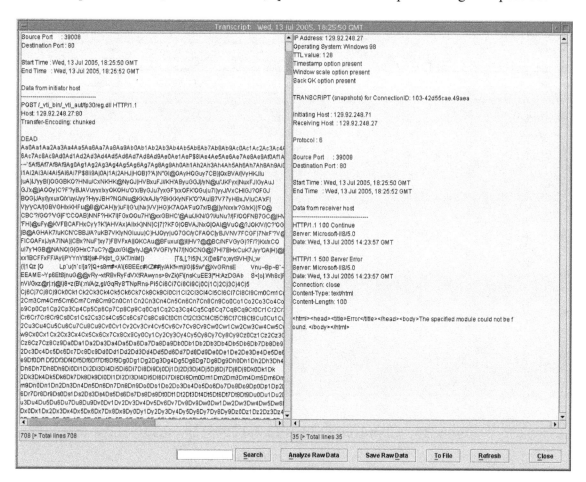

Figure 16: Captured Attempted Exploit 13 Jul 2005, 18:25:50GMT

4.5.2 RPC DCOM Exploit

Microsoft Windows platforms contain a potential vulnerability that may allow a remote attacker to execute arbitrary code. The issue is due to a flaw in the Remote Procedure Call (RPC) Distributed Component Object Model (DCOM) interface that does not properly sanitize remote requests. If an attacker sends a specially crafted message to the server, they may be able to crash the service or execute arbitrary code with SYSTEM privileges. This exploit was corrected by Microsoft patch KB828741 and is loaded on the system. This attempted exploit against a known patched system is in Figure 17 and was captured seven times.

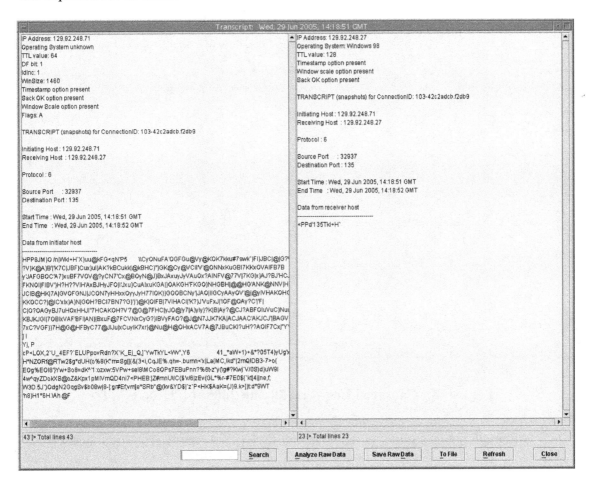

Figure 17: Captured Attempted Exploit 29 Jun 2005, 14:18:51GMT

4.6 Outlier Discussion

The research encountered three outliers that could not fit into any of the EPS categories. The first captured log data involved a session time out. The parameter of 900 seconds is set by the honeypot to close any connection when no activity occurs in the last 900 seconds. This data is shown in Figure 18 and was captured only once.

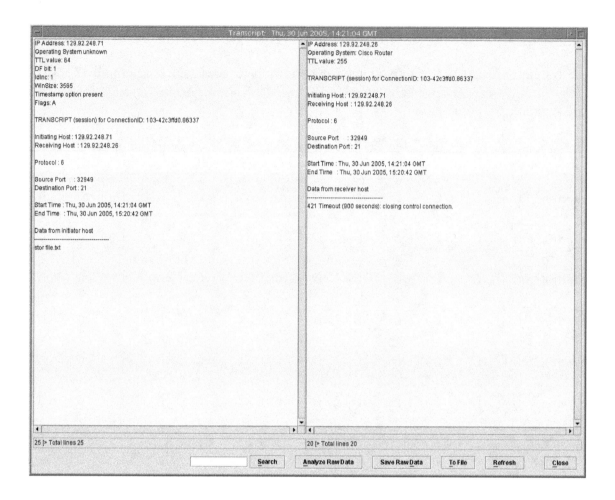

Figure 18: Captured Log Data 30 Jun 2005, 14:21:04 GMT

Although not an exploit, no session activity for 900 seconds (or any other set value) should cause alarm. This would not constitute a port scan or FTP banner retrieval so the EPS could not accurately predict this log data.

The remaining two outliers involved the RPC DCOM exploit. To determine relevancy of a patched exploit, the patch for RPC DCOM exploit (KB828741) was removed to see how the EPS would evaluate this exploit. Again, the RPC DCOM exploit allows a black hat to open a remote procedure call on an unknowing system. The exploit does not meet the criteria of bytes sent > 30 bytes, so the EPS would not predict this exploit. However, with the known Microsoft patch applied, this would be predicted to be

48

an exploit against a patched service. This exploit is shown in Figure 19 below and was

captured twice.

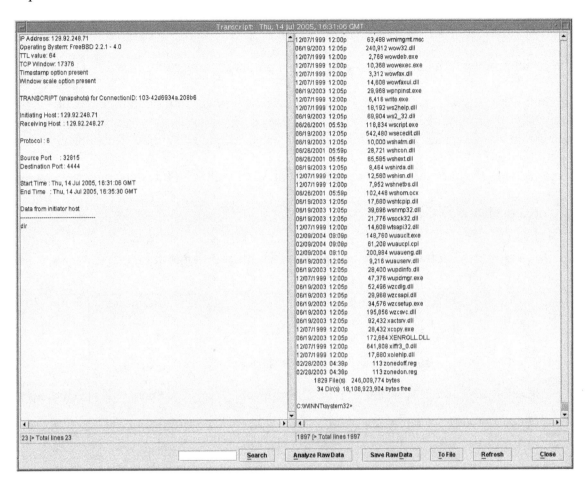

Figure 19: Captured Exploit 14 Jul 2005, 16:31:06GMT

Although not an outlier, the previously mentioned FrontPage exploits, 43

altogether, each had sent over 55,000 bytes to the honeypot. This met the EPS criteria of

> 30 bytes sent, but all were much more than the next most exploit or attempted exploit

of approximately 1,770 bytes sent. This may be attributable to the exploit being patched

and the "bot" attempting numerous operations before failing.

4.7 Analysis

As mentioned previously, a total of 8,444 lines of log data were captured during this research and a summary are depicted in Table 1 below. As expected, the overwhelming majority of log data were simple port scans (over 98 percent). The next amount were exploits against patched or non-offered services, although this may be somewhat skewed since the FrontPage exploit was attempted 43 times. Recognized exploits were the third most captured log data of 35. Finally, FTP banner retrievals were captured the least (17 times).

Table 1: Table of Log Data Captured (8,444 total)

Exploit	Exploit Against Patched or Non-Offered Services	FTP Banner Retrieval	Port Scan	Outliers
35 / 8,444	50 / 8,444	17 / 8,444	8,339 / 8,444	3 / 8,444

Using a 95-percent confidence level [Lil00], the upper level boundary, measured level and lower level boundary are listed in Table 2. The confidence interval shows enough measurements were taken to achieve a reasonable interval width (at 95% confidence).

Table 2: Confidence Level of Measurements Taken (at 95% level)

Confidence Intervals at 95%	Exploit	Exploit Against Patched or Non-Offered Services	FTP Banner Retrieval	Port Scan
Upper Level	.00529	.00768	.00310	.98901
Measured	.00414	.00627	.00225	.98698
Lower Level	.00299	.00486	.00140	.98495

4.8 EPS Accuracy

The EPS is intended only to be used on honeypots. The decision matrix simply would not work on a production-type system. As explained earlier, the honeypot is a non-production information system. A production-type system would have too much approved activity to capture and analyze. The false positives and false negatives would prove too enormous for any predictive analysis and the needed confidence level could not be attained. The network defender would spend too much time filtering the data. Much of the data would prove to be non-malicious and thus would waste valuable time. For all of these reasons, honeypots were invented to attract data that should always be considered malicious. To further enhance the honeypots, the EPS system provides an even better analytical tool to study actual exploits.

The EPS decision tree matrix criteria are summarized below:

- Recognized exploit equates to > 30 bytes sent and > 1,500 bytes received

- Attempted exploit equates to > 30 bytes sent and ≤ 1,500 bytes received

- FTP banner retrieval equates to ≤ 30 bytes sent and > 1,500 bytes received

- Port scan equates to ≤ 30 bytes sent and ≤ 1,500 bytes received.

Table 3 contains the statistics of the EPS success rates.

Table 3: Correct Predictions of the EPS

Recognized Exploit	Exploit Against Patched or Non-Offered Service	FTP Banner Retrieval	Port Scan
35 of 37	50 of 51	17 of 17	8,339 of 8,339
.9459	.9803	1.00	1.00

The EPS accurately predicted a port scan 100% of the time (8,339 of 8,339 events). The FTP Banner Retrieval also was accurately predicted 100% of the time (17 of 17 events). The port scan category proved the easiest to predict with the FTP banner retrieval proved second easiest to predict once the size of the banner was determined. Both of these categories do not reveal much system information to the black hat community and need no further preventive research probing for a computer deficiency.

The 35 recognized exploits were correctly predicted as exploits, with another two (the RPC DCOM exploit attempted with the applicable Microsoft patch removed) not predicted (95% success rate). This category proved the second most difficult to predict.

Further analysis uncovered the following characteristics of the 35 exploits:

	Bytes sent	Bytes received
Range:	37 – 1,376	1,700 – 5,073
Mean:	403	3,075
Median:	124	2,920

These values give an excellent representation for a network defender to monitor and further investigate these exploits down to the packet level as displayed in Figure 9.

The 50 exploits against patched or non-offered services were predicted successfully, with one (session time-out) not predicted for a 98% success rate. Again, these statistics may be somewhat skewed due to the FrontPage exploit executed 43 times in one period.

Further analysis uncovered the following characteristics of the 50 exploits:

	Bytes sent	Bytes received
Range:	150 – 57,116	60 – 347
Mean:	48,810	311
Mode:	56,472 (41 times)	347 (44 times)

The mode, versus the median, gives a better statistical representation of this category due to the number of the FrontPage exploits. Again, this provides a sound point for the system administrator to further investigate this captured log data. This category proved the most difficult to predict.

4.9 Summary

This chapter displayed the results of the data collected during this research. It is noted again the EPS should only be used on honeypots. It will not work to predict exploits on a production system. The data demonstrates the EPS is an excellent predictor of port scans and FTP banner retrieval. Furthermore, exploits and attempted exploits against patched or non-offered services are predicted at 95% confidence for exploits and for the attempted exploits. The statistics of the exploits and attempted exploits captured provide excellent reference criteria for the network defender to investigate certain log data down to the packet level. Conclusions and recommendations for further research are offered in the following chapter.

5. *Conclusions and Recommendations*

5.1 Goals of this Research Study

The goal of this research is simple. Using an accredited honeypot, employ an Exploit Prediction System (EPS) that will predict when an exploit has been transmitted to the honeypot. The EPS uses a decision tree matrix with as few criterion needed for successful prediction. The log data coming into the honeypot is not filtered and all data is interpreted and categorized.

5.2 EPS Uses

Most people involved in defending information networks only perform this crucial function as part of other work tasks. As more downsizing of our workforce occurs, the ability to spend time only on those packets of data predicted to cause harm is a force multiplier. The less time analyzing packets that are harmless enables the network defenders to perform other information assurance functions.

The amount of outside generated exploits was surprising. The anticipation was numerous exploits would target the honeypot. However, this proved to be false. The object of the research was to predict exploits. Where the exploits originated was not under test. Using Metapsploit [Moo04], several proven exploits were sent to the honeypots during the analysis and results phase and provided the needed research data.

5.3 Future Work

AFIT's honeypot has been accredited since August 2004 and this is the first thesis on honeypots. With the growing emergence of honeypots, the blackhat community now actively scans and detects potential honeypot systems and is not attacking those fingerprinted systems. In [Gup04], deceptive honeypots are thoroughly discussed as the next use for honeypots. This may prove to be an effective use, but may be too controversial for the Air Force to have connected to their information networks. Only further research can answer this question.

Potential research for this topic involves the Cyber Defense Exercise (CDX). This exercise is weeklong exercise that pits Red Team aggressors against Blue Team students in a battle to exploit and protect cyber resources and computer system services such as e-mail, web browsing, and database access. Participants include the military service academies, AFIT, and the Naval Postgraduate School. The National Security Agency and the Public Key Infrastructure (PKI) Office sponsor the CDX.

Before the weeklong exercise begins in the spring quarter, a prerequisite class (CSCE-528) is taught in the winter quarter. In conjunction with CSCE-528, a student could take on the honeypots as a special project and thoroughly evaluate how the honeypot could be used during the CDX. Early in the quarter, a temporary duty to the AFIWC, owners of the AFIT honeypot, could prove valuable. As the owner of the four honeypots, they are the authority and could provide much needed guidance for future research study. Any time spent with the owners of the system will only benefit the future research. The accredited honeypot is a valuable commodity and must be continually researched.

5.4 Summary

This research examines how honeypots are employed for use in Information Assurance in today's information networks. The EPS provides a simple, passive tool that allows only those packets of data predicted as an exploit to be analyzed further.

Honeypots can provide a deceptive defense tool in which the attackers are deceived into

believing they are intruding into a real production system. The correct deployment,

monitoring and analysis of honeypots help in increasing our understanding of attackers'

modes of operations and tools in details. With this knowledge, the goal of defending our

information networks can be achieved.

Appendix A. Abridged Listing of Captured Log Data

#	Start Day	Start Time (GMT)	Source IP	Dest IP	Source Port	Dest Port	Bytes Sent	Bytes Rxd	Pkts Sent	Pkts Rxd	Dur- ation	Prot- ocol
1	15-May-05	20:22:33	195.117.240.131	26	45932	21	0	1545	6	3	1	6
2	18-May-05	0:19:19	69.135.191.55	26	1641	21	13	1580	6	5	3	6
3	21-May-05	8:33:32	82.35.16.87	26	3113	21	0	1582	5	4	31	6
4	23-May-05	15:47:47	192.203.2.222	26	32780	21	67	1883	18	14	18	6
5	23-May-05	15:48:07	192.203.2.222	26	32781	21	62	1883	18	14	10	6
6	23-May-05	15:48:18	192.203.2.222	26	32782	21	87	3724	22	15	27	6
7	29-May-05	18:03:16	62.38.129.2	26	4367	21	0	1582	6	4	1	6
8	1-Jun-05	6:10:43	82.234.26.221	26	3091	21	0	1978	3	10	219	6
9	3-Jun-05	13:23:27	24.232.211.16	26	1382	21	0	1545	5	3	4	6
10	5-Jun-05	3:48:45	163.20.123.1	26	2100	21	0	1582	6	4	1	6
11	5-Jun-05	11:26:43	217.187.53.197	26	62747	21	175	3659	19	17	12	6
12	6-Jun-05	11:12:06	207.72.6.98	26	3926	21	124	1919	25	14	9	6
13	6-Jun-05	12:02:53	195.110.101.42	26	3633	21	0	1582	6	4	0	6
14	9-Jun-05	13:50:34	81.244.174.253	26	59631	21	46	3473	9	8	2	6
15	9-Jun-05	16:53:55	66.162.79.55	26	2789	21	185	3695	34	28	243	6
16	9-Jun-05	17:09:59	66.162.79.55	26	2806	21	66	1899	19	16	174	6
17	9-Jun-05	17:15:05	66.162.79.55	26	2810	21	397	4072	47	39	406	6
18	10-Jun-05	1:41:34	69.135.191.55	26	4319	21	13	1580	6	5	3	6
19	11-Jun-05	16:49:46	64.233.230.53	26	1429	21	0	1582	6	4	0	6
20	13-Jun-05	13:57:45	64.233.230.53	26	4397	21	684	5073	49	50	7	6
21	16-Jun-05	12:56:54	129.92.248.71	26	37607	1	300	0	1	0	0	17
22	16-Jun-05	12:57:42	129.92.248.71	26	47376	1	300	0	1	0	0	17

23	16-Jun-05	12:57:53	129.92.248.71	27	47376	1	300	0	1	0	0	17
24	17-Jun-05	17:12:37	81.137.93.81	26	6530	21	0	1582	6	4	0	6
25	19-Jun-05	15:43:09	84.160.148.118	26	2126	21	2	1658	7	5	0	6
26	23-Jun-05	18:00:16	129.92.248.71	26	32774	21	70	3528	22	16	847	6
27	23-Jun-05	18:00:33	129.92.248.71	26	32775	10173	0	0	2	1	830	6
28	23-Jun-05	18:37:03	129.92.248.71	26	32776	21	58	3325	19	13	12	6
29	29-Jun-05	13:51:28	129.92.248.71	27	32802	80	808	4289	7	5	0	6
30	29-Jun-05	13:51:29	129.92.248.71	27	32809	80	204	4246	7	5	0	6
31	29-Jun-05	14:02:31	129.92.248.71	27	32886	80	808	4289	7	5	0	6
32	29-Jun-05	14:02:31	129.92.248.71	27	32893	80	204	4246	7	5	0	6
33	29-Jun-05	14:14:16	129.92.248.71	27	32930	135	1770	60	7	4	0	6
34	29-Jun-05	14:18:51	129.92.248.71	27	32937	135	1770	60	7	4	1	6
35	29-Jun-05	16:00:17	129.92.248.71	26	32942	21	48	1812	15	11	496	6
36	29-Jun-05	16:08:44	129.92.248.71	26	32943	21	44	1700	13	11	938	6
37	30-Jun-05	00:28:17	129.92.250.39	27	1722	137	150	957	3	2	3	17
38	30-Jun-05	13:56:57	129.92.248.71	26	32943	21	6	0	2	1	0	6
39	30-Jun-05	13:57:12	129.92.248.71	26	32944	21	40	1804	15	13	283	6
40	30-Jun-05	14:02:09	129.92.248.71	26	32945	21	40	1804	14	12	28	6
41	30-Jun-05	14:02:59	129.92.248.71	26	32946	21	39	1803	14	10	36	6
42	30-Jun-05	14:03:51	129.92.248.71	26	32947	21	41	1804	15	13	18	6
43	30-Jun-05	14:04:37	129.92.248.71	26	32948	21	37	1804	14	12	18	6
44	30-Jun-05	14:05:05	129.92.248.71	26	32949	21	60	3463	23	16	59	6
45	30-Jun-05	14:05:22	129.92.248.71	26	32950	27883	0	845	4	3	0	6
46	30-Jun-05	14:21:04	129.92.248.71	26	32949	21	15	56	3	4	3578	6
47	6-Jul-05	19:36:23	192.203.1.218	26	4943	21	0	2327	2	14	931	6
48	7-Jul-05	00:17:55	192.203.1.218	26	1688	21	0	1780	6	7	53	6

59

49	8-Jul-05	22:42:09	4.43.98.63	26	3292	21	0	1582	6	4	1	6
50	10-Jul-05	14:45:58	68.143.90.52	26	3734	21	0	1582	6	4	0	6
51	10-Jul-05	22:47:26	69.25.82.229	26	3855	21	0	1582	6	4	1	6
52	13-Jul-05	14:31:51	129.92.248.71	27	32972	80	0	0	0	0	1	17
53	13-Jul-05	14:56:22	69.81.64.135	26	1274	21	105	3765	19	20	33	6
54	13-Jul-05	14:56:23	69.81.64.135	26	1275	21	146	3697	24	24	58	6
55	13-Jul-05	16:15:18	129.92.248.71	27	32972	80	1376	2920	7	4	0	6
56	13-Jul-05	16:20:41	129.92.248.71	27	32979	80	1014	2920	7	4	0	6
57	13-Jul-05	16:22:31	129.92.248.71	27	32981	80	1054	2920	7	4	0	6
58	13-Jul-05	16:24:09	129.92.248.71	27	32984	80	1316	2920	7	4	0	6
59	13-Jul-05	16:35:50	129.92.248.71	27	33020	80	1229	2920	7	4	0	6
60	13-Jul-05	16:38:36	129.92.248.71	27	33029	80	1229	2920	7	4	0	6
61	13-Jul-05	16:43:40	129.92.248.71	27	33032	80	1229	2920	7	4	0	6
62	13-Jul-05	17:38:55	129.92.248.71	27	33162	80	808	4289	7	5	0	6
63	13-Jul-05	17:38:58	129.92.248.71	27	33169	80	204	4246	7	5	0	6
64	13-Jul-05	17:42:11	129.92.248.71	27	33188	80	56472	347	43	16	2	6
65	13-Jul-05	17:43:13	129.92.248.71	27	33291	80	56472	347	43	16	2	6
66	13-Jul-05	17:44:15	129.92.248.71	27	33394	80	56472	347	43	16	2	6
67	13-Jul-05	17:45:17	129.92.248.71	27	33498	80	56472	347	43	16	2	6
68	13-Jul-05	17:46:19	129.92.248.71	27	33603	80	57116	347	43	16	2	6
69	13-Jul-05	17:47:21	129.92.248.71	27	33707	80	56472	347	43	16	2	6
70	13-Jul-05	17:48:22	129.92.248.71	27	33843	80	57116	347	43	16	2	6
71	13-Jul-05	17:49:23	129.92.248.71	27	33984	80	56472	347	43	16	2	6
72	13-Jul-05	17:50:25	129.92.248.71	27	34128	80	56472	347	43	16	2	6
73	13-Jul-05	17:51:26	129.92.248.71	27	34272	80	56472	347	43	16	2	6
74	13-Jul-05	17:52:27	129.92.248.71	27	34415	80	56472	347	43	16	2	6

75	13-Jul-05	17:53:29	129.92.248.71	27	34558	80	56472	347	43	16	2	6
76	13-Jul-05	17:54:30	129.92.248.71	27	34699	80	56472	347	43	16	2	6
77	13-Jul-05	17:55:32	129.92.248.71	27	34843	80	56472	347	43	17	2	6
78	13-Jul-05	17:56:34	129.92.248.71	27	34990	80	56472	347	43	16	2	6
79	13-Jul-05	17:57:36	129.92.248.71	27	35135	80	56472	347	43	16	2	6
80	13-Jul-05	17:58:37	129.92.248.71	27	35275	80	56472	347	43	16	2	6
81	13-Jul-05	17:59:39	129.92.248.71	27	35421	80	56472	347	43	16	2	6
82	13-Jul-05	18:00:41	129.92.248.71	27	35565	80	56472	347	43	16	2	6
83	13-Jul-05	18:01:43	129.92.248.71	27	35710	80	56472	347	43	16	2	6
84	13-Jul-05	18:02:44	129.92.248.71	27	35852	80	56472	347	43	16	2	6
85	13-Jul-05	18:03:46	129.92.248.71	27	36000	80	56472	347	43	16	2	6
86	13-Jul-05	18:04:48	129.92.248.71	27	36144	80	56472	347	43	16	2	6
87	13-Jul-05	18:05:50	129.92.248.71	27	36289	80	56472	347	43	16	2	6
88	13-Jul-05	18:06:51	129.92.248.71	27	36429	80	56472	347	43	16	2	6
89	13-Jul-05	18:07:53	129.92.248.71	27	36574	80	56472	347	43	16	2	6
90	13-Jul-05	18:08:55	129.92.248.71	27	36718	80	56472	347	43	16	2	6
91	13-Jul-05	18:09:57	129.92.248.71	27	36864	80	56472	347	43	16	2	6
92	13-Jul-05	18:10:58	129.92.248.71	27	37004	80	56472	347	43	16	2	6
93	13-Jul-05	18:12:00	129.92.248.71	27	37148	80	56472	347	43	16	2	6
94	13-Jul-05	18:13:01	129.92.248.71	27	37289	80	56472	347	43	16	2	6
95	13-Jul-05	18:14:03	129.92.248.71	27	37433	80	56472	347	43	16	2	6
96	13-Jul-05	18:15:05	129.92.248.71	27	37579	80	56472	347	43	16	2	6
97	13-Jul-05	18:16:06	129.92.248.71	27	37719	80	56472	347	43	16	2	6
98	13-Jul-05	18:17:08	129.92.248.71	27	37863	80	56472	347	43	16	2	6
99	13-Jul-05	18:18:09	129.92.248.71	27	38004	80	56472	347	43	16	2	6
100	13-Jul-05	18:19:11	129.92.248.71	27	38148	80	56472	347	43	16	2	6

101	13-Jul-05	18:20:12	129.92.248.71	27	38290	80	56472	347	43	16	2	6
102	13-Jul-05	18:21:14	129.92.248.71	27	38434	80	56472	347	43	16	2	6
103	13-Jul-05	18:22:16	129.92.248.71	27	38578	80	56472	347	43	16	2	6
104	13-Jul-05	18:23:17	129.92.248.71	27	38719	80	56472	347	43	16	2	6
105	13-Jul-05	18:24:19	129.92.248.71	27	38863	80	56472	347	43	16	2	6
106	13-Jul-05	18:25:50	129.92.248.71	27	39008	80	55024	347	43	19	2	6
107	13-Jul-05	18:48:37	129.92.248.71	27	39088	135	1770	60	8	5	1	6
108	13-Jul-05	18:48:38	129.92.248.71	27	39090	4444	0	105	4	2	0	6
109	14-Jul-05	16:21:50	129.92.248.71	27	32797	135	1770	60	8	5	1	6
110	14-Jul-05	16:21:51	129.92.248.71	27	32798	4444	34	96890	200	198	120	6
111	14-Jul-05	16:31:05	129.92.248.71	27	32813	135	1770	60	8	5	1	6
112	14-Jul-05	16:31:06	129.92.248.71	27	32815	4444	4	96742	131	161	264	6
113	14-Jul-05	16:49:42	129.92.248.71	27	32825	135	1770	152	9	5	1	6
114	14-Jul-05	16:57:30	129.92.248.71	27	32834	135	1770	152	9	5	1	6
115	16-Jul-05	15:31:58	209.123.110.70	26	17893	21	0	1582	6	4	0	6
………	…………	…………	………………………	……	…………	………	………	………	………	……………	……	……
8444	16-Jul-05	1:37:45	141.150.70.166	27	4901	10000	0	0	2	1	1	6

Appendix B. Listing of Captured Exploits by EPS Category

Exploits

#	Start Day	Start Time (GMT)	Source IP	Destination IP	Bytes Sent	Bytes Rxd	Description of Exploit
1	23-May-05	15:48:18	192.203.2.222	129.92.248.26	87	3724	NLST ~
2	23-May-05	15:47:47	192.203.2.222	129.92.248.26	67	1883	LIST
3	23-May-05	15:48:07	192.203.2.222	129.92.248.26	62	1883	LIST
4	5-Jun-05	11:26:43	217.187.53.197	129.92.248.26	175	3659	Grim's Ping
5	6-Jun-05	11:12:06	207.72.6.98	129.92.248.26	124	1919	LIST
6	9-Jun-05	17:15:05	66.162.79.55	129.92.248.26	397	4072	Grim's Ping
7	9-Jun-05	16:53:55	66.162.79.55	129.92.248.26	185	3695	NLST ~
8	9-Jun-05	13:50:34	81.244.174.253	129.92.248.26	46	3473	PASV
9	9-Jun-05	17:09:59	66.162.79.55	129.92.248.26	66	1899	LIST
10	13-Jun-05	13:57:45	64.233.230.53	129.92.248.26	684	5073	Grim's Ping
11	23-Jun-05	18:37:03	129.92.248.71	129.92.248.26	58	3325	PASV
12	23-Jun-05	18:00:16	129.92.248.71	129.92.248.26	70	3528	LIST
13	29-Jun-05	14:02:31	129.92.248.71	129.92.248.27	808	4289	Source Code Disclosure
14	29-Jun-05	13:51:28	129.92.248.71	129.92.248.27	808	4289	Source Code Disclosure
15	29-Jun-05	13:51:29	129.92.248.71	129.92.248.27	204	4246	Source Code Disclosure
16	29-Jun-05	14:02:31	129.92.248.71	129.92.248.27	204	4246	Source Code Disclosure
17	29-Jun-05	16:00:17	129.92.248.71	129.92.248.26	48	1812	SYST
18	29-Jun-05	16:08:44	129.92.248.71	129.92.248.26	44	1700	PASV
19	30-Jun-05	14:03:51	129.92.248.71	129.92.248.26	41	1804	SYST
20	30-Jun-05	14:02:09	129.92.248.71	129.92.248.26	40	1804	SYST
21	30-Jun-05	13:57:12	129.92.248.71	129.92.248.26	40	1804	SYST

63

22	30-Jun-05	14:02:59	129.92.248.71	129.92.248.26	39	1803 SYST
23	30-Jun-05	14:04:37	129.92.248.71	129.92.248.26	37	1804 SYST
24	30-Jun-05	14:05:05	129.92.248.71	129.92.248.26	60	3463 PASV
25	13-Jul-05	16:35:50	129.92.248.71	129.92.248.27	1229	2920 Printer Buffer Overflow
26	13-Jul-05	16:22:31	129.92.248.71	129.92.248.27	1054	2920 .HTR Bugger Overflow
27	13-Jul-05	16:20:41	129.92.248.71	129.92.248.27	1014	2920 .HTR Bugger Overflow
28	13-Jul-05	17:38:55	129.92.248.71	129.92.248.27	808	4289 Source Code Disclosure
29	13-Jul-05	16:15:18	129.92.248.71	129.92.248.27	1376	2920 .HTR Bugger Overflow
30	13-Jul-05	16:24:09	129.92.248.71	129.92.248.27	1316	2920 .HTR Bugger Overflow
31	13-Jul-05	16:43:40	129.92.248.71	129.92.248.27	1229	2920 Printer Buffer Overflow
32	13-Jul-05	16:38:36	129.92.248.71	129.92.248.27	1229	2920 Printer Buffer Overflow
33	13-Jul-05	14:56:23	69.81.64.135	129.92.248.26	146	3697 OPTS UTF8
34	13-Jul-05	17:38:58	129.92.248.71	129.92.248.27	204	4246 Source Code Disclosure
35	13-Jul-05	14:56:22	69.81.64.135	129.92.248.26	105	3765 OPTS UTF8

Attempted Exploits

#	Start Day	Start Time (GMT)	Source IP	Destination IP	Bytes Sent	Bytes Rxd	Description of Exploit
1	29-Jun-05	14:14:16	129.92.248.71	129.92.248.27	1770	60	RPC DCOM (patched)
2	29-Jun-05	14:18:51	129.92.248.71	129.92.248.27	1770	60	RPC DCOM (patched)
3	13-Jul-05	17:42:11	129.92.248.71	129.92.248.27	56472	347	FrontPage (non-offered)
4	13-Jul-05	17:43:13	129.92.248.71	129.92.248.27	56472	347	FrontPage (non-offered)
5	13-Jul-05	17:44:15	129.92.248.71	129.92.248.27	56472	347	FrontPage (non-offered)
6	13-Jul-05	17:45:17	129.92.248.71	129.92.248.27	56472	347	FrontPage (non-offered)
7	13-Jul-05	17:46:19	129.92.248.71	129.92.248.27	57116	347	FrontPage (non-offered)

8	13-Jul-05	17:47:21	129.92.248.71	129.92.248.27	56472	347	FrontPage (non-offered)
9	13-Jul-05	17:48:22	129.92.248.71	129.92.248.27	57116	347	FrontPage (non-offered)
10	13-Jul-05	17:49:23	129.92.248.71	129.92.248.27	56472	347	FrontPage (non-offered)
11	13-Jul-05	17:50:25	129.92.248.71	129.92.248.27	56472	347	FrontPage (non-offered)
12	13-Jul-05	17:51:26	129.92.248.71	129.92.248.27	56472	347	FrontPage (non-offered)
13	13-Jul-05	17:52:27	129.92.248.71	129.92.248.27	56472	347	FrontPage (non-offered)
14	13-Jul-05	17:53:29	129.92.248.71	129.92.248.27	56472	347	FrontPage (non-offered)
15	13-Jul-05	17:54:30	129.92.248.71	129.92.248.27	56472	347	FrontPage (non-offered)
16	13-Jul-05	17:55:32	129.92.248.71	129.92.248.27	56472	347	FrontPage (non-offered)
17	13-Jul-05	17:56:34	129.92.248.71	129.92.248.27	56472	347	FrontPage (non-offered)
18	13-Jul-05	17:57:36	129.92.248.71	129.92.248.27	56472	347	FrontPage (non-offered)
19	13-Jul-05	17:58:37	129.92.248.71	129.92.248.27	56472	347	FrontPage (non-offered)
20	13-Jul-05	17:59:39	129.92.248.71	129.92.248.27	56472	347	FrontPage (non-offered)
21	13-Jul-05	18:00:41	129.92.248.71	129.92.248.27	56472	347	FrontPage (non-offered)
22	13-Jul-05	18:01:43	129.92.248.71	129.92.248.27	56472	347	FrontPage (non-offered)
23	13-Jul-05	18:02:44	129.92.248.71	129.92.248.27	56472	347	FrontPage (non-offered)
24	13-Jul-05	18:03:46	129.92.248.71	129.92.248.27	56472	347	FrontPage (non-offered)
25	13-Jul-05	18:04:48	129.92.248.71	129.92.248.27	56472	347	FrontPage (non-offered)
26	13-Jul-05	18:05:50	129.92.248.71	129.92.248.27	56472	347	FrontPage (non-offered)
27	13-Jul-05	18:06:51	129.92.248.71	129.92.248.27	56472	347	FrontPage (non-offered)
28	13-Jul-05	18:07:53	129.92.248.71	129.92.248.27	56472	347	FrontPage (non-offered)
29	13-Jul-05	18:08:55	129.92.248.71	129.92.248.27	56472	347	FrontPage (non-offered)
30	13-Jul-05	18:09:57	129.92.248.71	129.92.248.27	56472	347	FrontPage (non-offered)
31	13-Jul-05	18:10:58	129.92.248.71	129.92.248.27	56472	347	FrontPage (non-offered)
32	13-Jul-05	18:12:00	129.92.248.71	129.92.248.27	56472	347	FrontPage (non-offered)
33	13-Jul-05	18:13:01	129.92.248.71	129.92.248.27	56472	347	FrontPage (non-offered)

34	13-Jul-05	18:14:03	129.92.248.71	129.92.248.27	56472	347	FrontPage (non-offered)
35	13-Jul-05	18:15:05	129.92.248.71	129.92.248.27	56472	347	FrontPage (non-offered)
36	13-Jul-05	18:16:06	129.92.248.71	129.92.248.27	56472	347	FrontPage (non-offered)
37	13-Jul-05	18:17:08	129.92.248.71	129.92.248.27	56472	347	FrontPage (non-offered)
38	13-Jul-05	18:18:09	129.92.248.71	129.92.248.27	56472	347	FrontPage (non-offered)
39	13-Jul-05	18:19:11	129.92.248.71	129.92.248.27	56472	347	FrontPage (non-offered)
40	13-Jul-05	18:20:12	129.92.248.71	129.92.248.27	56472	347	FrontPage (non-offered)
41	13-Jul-05	18:21:14	129.92.248.71	129.92.248.27	56472	347	FrontPage (non-offered)
42	13-Jul-05	18:22:16	129.92.248.71	129.92.248.27	56472	347	FrontPage (non-offered)
43	13-Jul-05	18:23:17	129.92.248.71	129.92.248.27	56472	347	FrontPage (non-offered)
44	13-Jul-05	18:24:19	129.92.248.71	129.92.248.27	56472	347	FrontPage (non-offered)
45	13-Jul-05	18:25:50	129.92.248.71	129.92.248.27	55024	347	FrontPage (non-offered)
46	13-Jul-05	18:48:37	129.92.248.71	129.92.248.27	1770	60	RPC DCOM (patched)
47	14-Jul-05	16:21:50	129.92.248.71	129.92.248.27	1770	60	RPC DCOM (patched)
48	14-Jul-05	16:31:05	129.92.248.71	129.92.248.27	1770	60	RPC DCOM (patched)
49	14-Jul-05	16:49:42	129.92.248.71	129.92.248.27	1770	152	RPC DCOM (patched)
50	14-Jul-05	16:57:30	129.92.248.71	129.92.248.27	1770	152	RPC DCOM (patched)

FTP Banner Retrievals

#	Start Day	Start Time (GMT)	Source IP	Destination IP	Bytes Sent	Bytes Rxd	Description of Exploit
1	18-May-05	0:19:19	69.135.191.55	129.92.248.26	13	1580	FTP Banner Retrieval
2	21-May-05	8:33:32	82.35.16.87	129.92.248.26	0	1582	FTP Banner Retrieval
3	29-May-05	18:03:16	62.38.129.2	129.92.248.26	0	1582	FTP Banner Retrieval
4	1-Jun-05	6:10:43	82.234.26.221	129.92.248.26	0	1978	FTP Banner Retrieval

5	3-Jun-05	13:23:27	24.232.211.16	129.92.248.26	0	1545 FTP Banner Retrieval
6	5-Jun-05	3:48:45	163.20.123.1	129.92.248.26	0	1582 FTP Banner Retrieval
7	6-Jun-05	12:02:53	195.110.101.42	129.92.248.26	0	1582 FTP Banner Retrieval
8	10-Jun-05	1:41:34	69.135.191.55	129.92.248.26	13	1580 FTP Banner Retrieval
9	11-Jun-05	16:49:46	64.233.230.53	129.92.248.26	0	1582 FTP Banner Retrieval
10	17-Jun-05	17:12:37	81.137.93.81	129.92.248.26	0	1582 FTP Banner Retrieval
11	19-Jun-05	15:43:09	84.160.148.118	129.92.248.26	2	1658 FTP Banner Retrieval
12	6-Jul-05	19:36:23	192.203.1.218	129.92.248.26	0	2327 FTP Banner Retrieval
13	7-Jul-05	00:17:55	192.203.1.218	129.92.248.26	0	1780 FTP Banner Retrieval
14	8-Jul-05	22:42:09	4.43.98.63	129.92.248.26	0	1582 FTP Banner Retrieval
15	10-Jul-05	14:45:58	68.143.90.52	129.92.248.26	0	1582 FTP Banner Retrieval
16	10-Jul-05	22:47:26	69.25.82.229	129.92.248.26	0	1582 FTP Banner Retrieval
17	16-Jul-05	15:31:58	209.123.110.70	129.92.248.26	0	1582 FTP Banner Retrieval

Port Scans

#	Start Day	Start Time (GMT)	Source IP	Destination IP	Bytes Sent	Bytes Rxd	Description of Exploit
1	23-Jun-05	0:04:42	67.115.193.178	129.92.248.27	0	0	Port Scan
2	23-Jun-05	18:00:33	129.92.248.71	129.92.248.26	0	0	Port Scan
3	30-Jun-05	14:05:22	129.92.248.71	129.92.248.26	0	845	Port Scan (ACLs)
4	13-Jul-05	14:31:51	129.92.248.71	129.92.248.27	0	0	Port Scan
5	13-Jul-05	18:48:38	129.92.248.71	129.92.248.27	0	105	Port Scan (Windows)
....	....	....	....	....	..	....	....
8339	10-Jul-05	23:49:48	209.26.128.174	129.92.248.26	0	0	Port Scan

Bibliography

[AFI04a]   Air Force Information Warfare Center (AFIWC), Technology Application Branch. *CNDRS ASIM Gateway Environment (CAGE) System Administrator's Manual.* http://afiwcweb.lackland.af.mil/home/index.cfm, Nov 2004.

[AFI04b]   Air Force Information Warfare Center (AFIWC), Technology Application Branch. *FTP Server Honeypot System Administrator's Manual.* http://afiwcweb.lackland.af.mil/home/index.cfm, Nov 2004.

[Bau02]   Reto Baumann. *Honeypots.* Diploma Thesis in Computer Science from the Swiss Federal Institute of Technology. https://www.rbaumann.net/download/diplomathesis.pdf, Feb 2002.

[Bus05]   SrA Todd Bush. *Training Key to Success.* Intercom, Journal of the Air Force C4ISR Community, Jul 2005.

[Che05]   Capt David Cheboya. *Advanced Network Intrusion Detection System (NIDS) Evasion Techniques and Solutions.* Air Force Institute of Technology Thesis, Mar 2005.

[Che91]   Bill Cheswick. *An Evening With Berferd In Which A Cracker is Lured, Endured, and Studied.* AT&T Bell Laboratories, http://www.tracking-hackers.com/papers/bereferd.pdf, 1991.

[Gup04]   Nirbhay Gupta. *Improving the Effectiveness of Deceptive Honeynets Through an Empirical Learning Approach.* SecurityDocs.com. http://www.infosecwriters.com/text_resources/pdf/Gupta_Honeynets.pdf, Mar 2004.

[Hon00a]   The Honeynet Project. *Know Your Enemy: The Motives and Psychology of the Black-Hat Community.* http://project.honeynet.org, Jun 2000.

[Hon00b]   The Honeynet Project. *Know Your Enemy: The Tools and Methodologies of the Script Kiddie.* http://project.honeynet.org, Jul 2000.

[Hon02]   The Honeynet Project Team. *Looking Under the Black Hat.* Security Management Journal, Jan 2002 pg. 39-43.

[Hon03a]   The Honeynet Project. *Know Your Enemy: A Profile: Automated Credit Card Fraud.* http://project.honeynet.org, Jun 2003.

[Hon03b]   The Honeynet Project. *Know Your Enemy: A Kernel Based Capture Tool.* http://project.honeynet.org, Nov 2003.

[Hon03c]   The Honeynet Project. *Know Your Enemy: Targeting a More Sophisticated Clientele.* http://project.honeynet.org, Nov 2003.

[Hon04a]   The Honeynet Project. *Know Your Enemy – Learning About Security Threats.* Addison-Wesley, 2004.

[Hon04b]   The Honeynet Project. *Know Your Enemy: Honeynets in Universities.* http://project.honeynet.org, Apr 2004.

[Hon05]   Developments of the HoneyD Virtual Honeypot, WWW Page URL http://www.honeyd.org, Aug 2005.

[Jtf04]   Joint Task Force-Global Network Operations. http://www.cert.mil. Accessed Jan-Sep 2004.

[Lil04]   David J. Lilja. *Measuring Computer Performance, A Practitioner's Guide.* Cambridge University Press, 2000.

[LLO03]   John Levine, Richard LaBella, Henry Owen, Didier Contis and Brian Culver. *The Use of Honeynets to Detect Exploited Systems Across Large Enterprise Networks.* Proceedings of the 2003 IEEE Workshop on Information Assurance, June 2003.

[LM04]   Timothy Lacey and Scott McIntyre. *Computer Network Defense and Response System (CNDRS).* Visitor briefing developed for the Center for Information Security Education and Research (CISER). Sep 2004.

[Mcc03]   Bill McCarty. *Botnets: Big and Bigger.* IEEE Security and Privacy Magazine, Jul/Aug 2003, pg. 87-90.

[Mid01]   James Middleton. *Hackers Launch Cyber Jihad on US.* VNU Business Publications, http://vnunet.com/news/1126240, Oct 2001.

[Moo04]   H.D. Moore, Metasploit Framework Documentation, http://www.metasploit.com, 2004.

[Mit02]   The "MIDAS" Touch: MITRE's Unique Intrusion Detection and Analysis Capability. WWW Page URL http://www.mitre.org/news/digest/defense_intelligence/12_02/di_midas_touch.html, 2002.

[MSK03]   Stuart McClure, Joel Scambray and George Kurts. *Hacking Exposed.* Fourth Edition. McGraw-Hill, 2003.

[NFR05]   Security Resource Center, WWW Page URL
             http://www.afr.com/resource/backOfficer.php, 2005.

[OSV05]   The Open Source Vulnerability Data Base, WWW Page URL
             http://www.osvdb.org, 2005.

[Pet05]   Personal interview with Dr. Gilbert Peterson at Air Force Institute of
             Technology at Wright Patterson Air Force, OH, May 2005.

[Sec01]   FTPD Glob Heap Corruption. WWW Page URL
             http://www.securityspace.com/smysecure/catid.html?id=10821, 2001.

[Sec04]   Secunia Stay Secure. WWW Page URL http://www.secunia.com, 2005.

[Spi03a]   Lance Spitzner. *Honeypots – Tracker Hackers.* Addison Wesley, 2003.

[Spi03b]   Lance Spitzner. *The Honeynet Project: Trapping the Hackers.* IEEE
             Security and Privacy Magazine, Mar/Apr 2003, pg 15-23.

[Sto89]   Clifford Stoll. *The Cuckoo's Egg.* Doubleday Publishing. 1989.

[Sym05]   Symantec Decoy Server, WWW page URL
             http://www.enterprisesecurity.symantec.com/products, 2005.

[Tar04]   Jim Taratino. *Information Assurance for the Deployed Warfighter.*
             Intercom: Journal of the Air Force C4 Community Magazine, Oct 2004,
             pg. 12-13.

[Tor02]   Captain Jesus Torres, Jr., USMC. *The Design and Architecture of 2nd
             Generation Honeynets Using Network Deception.* Naval Postgraduate
             School Thesis, Sep 2002.

[ZZQ03]   Feng Zhang, Shijie Zhou, Zhiguang Qin and Jinde Liu. *Honeypot: A
             Supplemented Active Defense System for Network Security.* Proceedings
             of the 4th International Conference held on 27-29 Aug 03, pg. 231-235.

www.ingramcontent.com/pod-product-compliance
Lightning Source LLC
LaVergne TN
LVHW060147070326
832902LV00018B/2993